Helen Keller
GIRL OF COURAGE

Helen Keller
GIRL OF COURAGE

By Francene Sabin and Joanne Mattern
Illustrated by Jean Meyer

SCHOLASTIC INC.
New York   Toronto   London   Auckland   Sydney
Mexico City   New Delhi   Hong Kong   Buenos Aires

ISBN-13: 978-0-439-66043-3
ISBN-10: 0-439-66043-2

12 11 10 9 8 7 6 5 4 3   7 8 9 10 11/0

Printed in the U.S.A.   23
First printing, March 2006

CONTENTS

CHAPTER 1:
A Terrible Illness

The sweet scent of honeysuckle floated through the air. The sun was warm. A chickadee hopped along a tree branch, singing. A golden-haired girl, just one year old, sat on a blanket in the grass and looked up at the bird. She laughed at its merry, piping song. Then she looked down at the doll in her lap. She liked its orange woolen hair and button eyes.

"Helen, come to Mama, darling."

The little girl turned around. She saw her mother standing nearby, arms outstretched.

"Ma-ma. Ma-ma," said the child. A smile

1

shining on her face, little Helen stood and toddled to her mother's arms.

"Happy birthday!" said Mrs. Keller. "One year old today! Come in and see the presents everyone has brought for you."

The presents looked pretty in their shiny wrappings, but Helen had eyes for just one thing: the birthday cake. It had white icing and pink sugar roses with mint-green leaves. Best of all, it had one tiny candle glowing on top. The flame danced and fluttered. The little girl giggled with delight.

Helen Keller would never see another birthday candle or ever again hear her family sing "Happy Birthday" to her. For when she was nineteen months old, she suffered a terrible sickness. Her fever raged for days. Doctors could do nothing to help her. It was the winter of 1882, and doctors didn't know a lot of things they know now. They also did not have the special medicines called antibiotics, which are used today to treat many illnesses. The only thing

they could do for Helen was to make her comfortable and pray for her recovery.

Helen did recover. Her parents rejoiced, but their joy did not last long. The day after Helen's fever broke, Mrs. Keller noticed something strange. When she moved her hand in front of the little girl's eyes, Helen did not blink. She did not seem to see her mother's hand at all.

A few days later, Mrs. Keller noticed something else. When she called Helen's name, her daughter did not answer. Mrs. Keller stood near her daughter and shouted at her, but Helen did not respond. She clapped her hands and made loud noises, but Helen sat motionless. A doctor later confirmed what Mrs. Keller already knew was true. Helen's fever had left her totally blind and deaf.

At first, Mr. and Mrs. Keller hoped this nightmare would pass. Mr. Keller would stand near his daughter and clap his hands together sharply. But Helen did not turn toward the sound. Mrs.

Keller would hold up an oil lamp. But Helen did not turn toward the light.

Helen's parents were devastated. At that time, people who were blind or deaf had a very limited future. Many were sent to live in institutions. They did not go to school, find good jobs, go to parties, or get married. Helen's parents had dreamed of a bright future for their daughter, but now it seemed that she would have no life at all. Mrs. Keller took the news especially hard. She later wrote, "Fear ambushed the joy in my heart when I was twenty-four and left me for dead."

For the next six years, the Kellers tried everything they could think of to help Helen. They took her to doctors all over the country. They tried many different treatments. Nothing worked. Finally, they accepted the fact that Helen would be blind and deaf forever. Because she could not hear, Helen also would not be able to speak.

Many people told the Kellers they should put Helen in an institution. They said she would never have a normal life. But the Kellers refused. Their daughter would live at home with them.

Helen's parents accepted the sad truth of their daughter's blindness and deafness. But when friends told them that their child was feeble-minded, they could not accept that. They knew that Helen was bright. And they never gave up hope that, one day, she would show the world just how smart she was.

CHAPTER 2:
Joy and Frustration

The Kellers did their best to make Helen's life full and happy. They gave her lots of love and attention. They let her roam freely around their home in Tuscumbia, Alabama. She ran through the fields with Belle, the family setter. She rode the small pony that lived in the barn behind the house.

The little girl loved the smell of flowers in the garden, fresh bread baking in the kitchen, and her mother's perfume. She loved the taste of cold ice cream and hot biscuits. And she loved the rough feel of tree bark under her fingertips and the silkiness of Belle's fur.

There were moments of happiness, like tiny islands in a vast ocean. But mostly, Helen's life was like being alone in a silent, dark room.

Whatever she felt was locked inside. Her love had nowhere to go. Her anger had nowhere to go. Her fears had nowhere to go.

Helen could not communicate with anyone, and this frustrated her very much. She knew she was different from others, but she could not understand why. When she grew up, Helen described her confusion. "Sometimes I stood between two persons . . . and touched their lips. I could not understand and was vexed. I moved my lips and gesticulated frantically without result. This made me so angry at times that I kicked and screamed till I was exhausted."

Helen's tantrums grew worse as she got bigger

and stronger. She broke dishes. She grabbed food away from people. She hit, kicked, and scratched. Once she locked her mother in the pantry for several hours. Another time, she chased her grandmother around the parlor and pinched her. Helen's parents did not know how to stop Helen's wild behavior. They felt sorry for Helen and could not bear to discipline her. So they let her do whatever she wanted, even though that meant Helen often acted like a wild animal.

CHAPTER 3:
Looking for Answers

When Helen was five, Mrs. Keller read about a woman named Laura Bridgman, who was also deaf and blind. She had been taught to read and write, and to "talk" to people by using a finger alphabet. Her teacher was Dr. Samuel Gridley Howe, of the Perkins Institution and Massachusetts School for the Blind, in Boston, Massachusetts.

Laura Bridgman's story gave the Kellers hope that something could be done for Helen. So, as soon as they could, they took her to Baltimore, Maryland, to see an eye specialist.

The doctor examined Helen, and said, "I'm sorry, her condition will never change. But she can learn a lot of things. There is nothing wrong with her mind. I have a suggestion to make."

"What is that?" Mrs. Keller asked. "We'll do anything that might help Helen."

"I think you should take her to Washington, D.C., to see Dr. Bell. He has had great success teaching deaf people."

The Kellers took a train to the nation's capital. There, they went to see Dr. Alexander Graham Bell. Today, Dr. Bell is remembered mainly as the inventor of the telephone. In those days, however, he was best known for the school he had founded, where teachers were trained to instruct deaf students.

Long train rides, strange hotels, meeting many new people — it all confused and frightened Helen. But Dr. Bell was very gentle. He sat her on his knees and guided her hands to his face. She felt his droopy mustache and heavy beard. Then he held his gold pocket watch against her cheek. She could feel the steady *tick-tock* and she nodded her head in rhythm with it.

Helen was not afraid of this kind man. She sat still while he examined her. Then he told the Kellers, "I am certain that this clever little girl can be taught to communicate with others."

Dr. Bell suggested that Mr. Keller write to the Perkins Institution, where Laura Bridgman had learned the finger language. Perhaps the director, Michael Anagnos, could find the right teacher for Helen.

Mr. Keller did write the letter and soon received an answer. Mr. Anagnos knew of a young woman who would make a perfect teacher and companion for Helen. Her name was Annie Sullivan.

Annie was twenty years old and had graduated from Perkins earlier that year. Her eyesight was poor, but she was not blind. Annie desperately wanted a job and was thrilled when Mr. Keller offered her twenty-five dollars a month plus room and board. She quickly accepted the job.

18

CHAPTER 4:
Teacher

Arrangements were made quickly, and Annie Sullivan arrived in Tuscumbia on March 3, 1887. Mrs. Keller met her at the train, and they rode back to the house in a horse-drawn carriage.

Helen did not know why there was so much excitement in the house. But something told her that today was very special. When she could not find her mother anywhere, Helen went to the front door. She stood there and waited.

The carriage drew up in front of the house, and Annie Sullivan got her first look at Helen. The young girl's dress was dirty. Her light-brown curls were tangled and uncombed. She stood tense and frightened, like a startled fawn in the forest.

Mr. Keller helped Annie down from the carriage. She began to walk up the wooden steps to the front porch. Helen felt the vibrations made by the footsteps and rushed at the stranger.

Annie caught her before the wild charge knocked both of them down the steps.

Annie knelt and put her arms around Helen. She smiled as the child's fingers felt her eyes, her nose, her hair, and her hat. When Helen was finished "meeting" the stranger, Annie took her hand and they walked into the house, side by side.

Their first days together were not easy. Annie was unhappy about Helen's wild behavior. The child was allowed to walk around the dining

table, sticking her fingers into everybody's food and taking whatever she wanted. She was very rough with Mildred, her baby sister, and with the dog, Belle. Helen would not let anybody comb her hair or wash her face and hands. And she would fly into a fierce rage when anyone tried to make her do something she didn't want to do.

Annie understood why Helen acted this way. Her parents felt so sorry for their unfortunate little girl that they could not bear to punish her, no matter what she did. They never made her obey rules.

Annie knew she had to tame this wild young girl. Helen had to learn to get along with other people. Until she did, she could not be taught anything.

CHAPTER 5:
Difficult Lessons

First, Annie tried to win Helen's trust. She gave the little girl a doll that had been sent to Helen by the children at the Perkins Institution.

Helen ran her hands over the doll. She smiled and hugged it tightly. A moment later, Helen felt Annie take hold of her right hand. She felt fingers fluttering and tapping on her palm. The tapping stopped. Then again she felt the same tap-flutters on her palm. And again. Helen was puzzled.

Annie was using a special finger language to spell
d-o-l-l in Helen's hand. She spelled it over and over.
But Helen did not understand what was happening. Annie took the doll away from Helen. She
meant to give it back after Helen spelled the word
d-o-l-l. But Helen thought Annie was taking the
doll away forever. She threw herself on the floor,
kicking and screaming.

Annie feared she had made a terrible mistake.
She ran down to the kitchen and asked the cook
for a slice of cake. Annie took the cake back to the
room where Helen was.

Annie took the piece of cake and touched

Helen's hand to it. Helen loved cake and started to grab it. Annie stopped her. With one hand, she held Helen's left hand so that it just touched the cake. At the same time, she spelled *c-a-k-e* into Helen's right hand. She spelled it again and again.

Helen scowled. She started to pull away. Then, suddenly, she stopped. Putting her fingers in Annie's hand, she very slowly spelled *c-a-k-e*. Annie was thrilled with Helen's quick response. She gave Helen the cake. The young girl ate it happily.

As soon as Helen finished her last crumb, she felt Annie guide her left hand over the doll. Helen wanted it; it felt so soft and cuddly. She tugged at it. But Annie didn't let her have it. Then Helen put her fingers in Annie's hand and spelled *d-o-l*. Annie guided Helen's fingers through the second *l*, then placed the doll in Helen's arms. A smile spread across Helen's face.

This first success filled Annie with joy. Helen

could learn! Now there was much to do. They began the next morning. Annie gave Helen milk and spelled *m-i-l-k* at the same time. She spelled *c-a-t*, while Helen petted the purring pet. And in this way, one new word followed another as the days flew by.

Although Annie's pupil showed great promise, there was still the problem of trying to discipline her. Sometimes Helen was very friendly. But at other times, she had tantrums. She would kick and punch, shove people or throw things, until she got her way. Annie had to stop that. She knew that Mr. and Mrs. Keller never would. So she asked them to let her have complete control over Helen. They agreed.

At breakfast the next morning, Annie made Helen sit in her own chair at the table. She would not let the child take food from anyone else. The first time Helen tried to, Annie slapped her hand. Helen pinched Annie. Annie slapped her hand again. Helen stamped her feet in fury.

Annie dragged Helen to her own chair and made her sit in it. Then she put a spoon in the child's hand and guided it to her food-filled plate. Helen threw the spoon on the floor. Annie made her pick it up.

Mrs. Keller was crying, and Mr. Keller's face was a mask of pain. They hated to see their Helen suffer so. "She can't help herself," Mrs. Keller said. "She doesn't know better."

"We can help her to know better," Annie said in a gentle voice.

The Kellers left the dining room. Annie locked the door behind them. Then the battle really began. Annie was determined — Helen would learn to sit in her chair, eat properly, and fold her napkin when she was finished.

Helen walked around, touching every chair. When she found that her parents were gone, she crawled under the table. Annie pulled her out and sat her in her chair. Helen picked up the food with her fingers. Annie wiped them clean

and gave her a spoon. Helen tried to drop it, but Annie wouldn't let her. Helen struggled. Annie was stronger.

Helen finally gave in and ate with the spoon. Even so, the battle was not over. When she finished eating, Helen tossed her napkin on the table. Annie made her pick it up, fold it, and place it beside her plate. A moment later, Helen flung the napkin to the floor. Annie made her get out of the chair, pick it up, and fold it again. Helen was sobbing, but she would not give in. Neither would Annie. At last, the napkin remained on the table, folded neatly. Only then did Annie unlock the door and let Helen out.

That night, Annie cried herself to sleep. She hated being harsh with Helen. She really loved the child and wanted to be her friend. But first, she knew, Helen would have to depend on her. Only then could the real learning begin.

Annie's complete control over Helen was the only way she could teach the little girl to behave — and to learn. The Kellers did not agree at first, but after a week, they finally decided to try Annie's plan. Annie and Helen moved into a small cottage near the Kellers' home. For the next two weeks, Helen and Annie spent all their time together.

The battle of wills went on. But each day was a bit easier than the day before. One morning, Helen brought her comb to Annie for the first time. The next day, she let Annie get her ready for bed, then tuck her in for the night. And she was learning, too, to sew an apron for her doll, to crochet, to string beads, to "say" new words in finger talk.

Annie was delighted. At last, Helen liked her and trusted her. By the time they returned to the main house two weeks later, Helen was a different child.

Yet there was something missing. Helen learned to make the words in finger talk, but she didn't *know* that they were words. She didn't know how to use them the way other people did.

CHAPTER 6:

W-a-t-e-r!

Then, one day, Helen and Annie found the key that opened the door to the world for Helen Keller! It was April 5, 1887.

Annie described the moment of discovery in a letter to a friend. She wrote: "We went out to the pump house, and I made Helen hold her hands under the spout while I pumped. I spelled *w-a-t-e-r* into her free hand. . . . The word coming so close upon the sensation of cold water rushing over her hand seemed to startle her. She dropped the mug and stood transfixed. A new

light came into her face. She spelled *w-a-t-e-r* several times."

Then Helen reached down and touched the ground. Annie spelled *g-r-o-u-n-d* in her hand. Helen looked excited and pointed at Annie. Annie spelled *t-e-a-c-h-e-r*. Helen understood. And from that day on, she always called Annie Sullivan by the name *Teacher*.

Now Helen pointed to herself. Annie spelled *H-e-l-e-n K-e-l-l-e-r*. Helen trembled with joy. She had a name, too!

Helen grabbed Annie's hand, and they flew into

the house together. They found Mrs. Keller. Helen burrowed into her mother's arms, while Annie spelled m-o-t-h-e-r on her hand. Helen understood, and she nodded her head. Tears of thankfulness spilled from Mrs. Keller's eyes.

Helen couldn't learn enough to satisfy her thirst for words that day. She moved quickly around the house, touching things, learning the word for each one.

Years later, Helen wrote, "It was as if I had come back to life after being dead. . . . Delicious sensations rippled through me, and strange sweet things that were locked up in my heart began to sing."

Helen was up with the sun the next morning, ready to learn more. She woke Annie with a hug and a kiss — and a tug of hands that said, "Hurry! Get up!"

It took a while for Helen to get dressed, but not because she made it a battle. As she put on each piece of clothing, she wanted to know all

about it. Now she knew she wore a *dress*, and that it had *sleeves*, a *skirt*, *buttons*, *buttonholes*, a *collar*, and a *belt*.

That was just the beginning. Words poured into Helen. She touched trees and grass and stones, and learned their names. She held an egg in her hand and felt a baby chick break through the shell and hatch. Then Annie's fingers told her all about the miracle of life she had felt.

Her teacher taught Helen to hop and skip and jump, telling her the word for each action. They did the same thing with foods, people's names, animals, flowers, furniture — everything in the world around them.

CHAPTER 7:
A Thirst for Knowledge

Annie wanted Helen to feel free and happy. So they spent most of their days outside, doing their lessons under a big tree in the garden. Helen learned geography by making maps with wet dirt. She shaped mountains and valleys, islands and rivers, even whole continents. She learned the shape of the earth by holding an orange. Annie could hardly keep pace with Helen's endless desire for "more words."

If Helen could read, Annie decided, she would learn much faster. So Annie taught her to read braille. This is a way of printing words by using

raised dots on paper. It was invented by Louis Braille in 1829, so that blind people could read by touch.

Annie had Helen feel the braille letter *a* with the fingers of one hand, while *a* was finger-spelled into her other hand. Then *b* . . . and *c*. Helen mastered the braille alphabet right away. Annie brought her books written in braille. Helen loved them so much that she always slept with one in her bed.

Next, Annie taught Helen how to write in braille. Before long, Helen was writing stories,

notes to Teacher, and letters to the blind children at the Perkins Institution.

Mr. and Mrs. Keller were thrilled at Helen's progress. "You have worked a miracle," Mr. Keller told Annie.

"The miracle is Helen," Annie insisted. "She can learn anything. Why, right now, we are working on ordinary writing. You will soon be reading her letters yourself."

Annie taught Helen to write by copying raised letters from a set of alphabet cards she had brought with her from Perkins. She also used a tool called a writing board. The writing board had grooved lines in it. When a piece of paper was laid on top of the board, the grooves could be felt through the paper. This helped Helen write letters in a straight line. Helen also used her left hand to guide her right hand across the paper as she wrote. Annie taught Helen to write her letters in a squared-off style called square-hand script. Helen's handwriting was very neat, even though she could not see what she was writing.

CHAPTER 8:
School Days

Helen wanted to learn, learn, learn. Annie did her best, but she could see that Helen needed more than she could give her. Around the same time, Michael Anagnos, the director of Perkins, invited Helen to visit the school. Helen was eager to go, and Annie was eager to visit Boston and show Helen the school she had attended. So, in the spring of 1888, they took a train to Boston. There, at the Perkins Institution, Helen went to a real school for the first time.

Annie sat next to her in every class, spelling out the teacher's words in Helen's hand. Helen

learned geography, zoology, Latin, German, arithmetic, English, Greek, and French. She didn't *have* to study all those subjects, she *wanted* to!

From eight o'clock in the morning until six o'clock at night, Helen went to classes. She stopped only for lunch and for an hour of play with other children in the gym. It was very tiring for Annie, who never left her side, but Helen thrived on it.

Helen loved being at Perkins. For the first time, she was surrounded by children who were blind, just like she was. She communicated with them by using the manual alphabet — spelling words into their hands — and was thrilled that they understood her. At home, only a few people in her family had learned the alphabet and could understand Helen. Helen loved playing games with her new friends. For the first time, she did not feel different from everyone around her.

Perkins held another treasure for Helen. The school had the largest collection of materials for the blind in the United States. Helen loved books, but she had already read all of the braille books Annie had brought to Alabama. She was thrilled to discover a huge number of braille books in the Perkins library and spent hours reading them.

When Helen was ten, she read about a blind, deaf girl in Norway. That girl had learned to speak words out loud. Helen wanted to do the same thing. Annie took her to the Horace Mann School for the Deaf in Boston. There, a teacher named Sarah Fuller began working with Helen. First, Helen placed her hand on Miss Fuller's mouth. She felt the way words are formed. Then Helen tried to copy this with her mouth.

Helen could not hear her own voice, so she could not know if her words sounded the way they should. Annie worked with her, day and night. Their reward came when Helen said, "It is warm," in a clear voice. And when they went to Tuscumbia for summer vacation, Helen's family

received a beautiful surprise.

The Kellers were waiting at the train station. Helen, prettier than ever, stepped down to the platform. Very proudly, she said, "Mother, I am not dumb now. Mildred, I love you. Father, I am glad to be home."

This was a moment the Kellers would never forget. Although Helen's speech would always be hard to understand, hearing her voice was more than the Keller's ever could have imagined.

It was a wonderful summer vacation. Then Helen and Annie returned to school in Boston. And this is how they spent each year as Helen grew into her teens.

CHAPTER 9:
A New Dream

By the time she was ten years old, Helen had become famous all over the country. Her remarkable story was published in magazines and newspapers, and she was called "the wonder child." Helen's fame sometimes annoyed her parents, who often had to chase away reporters who showed up uninvited at the family's home. However, Helen and Annie were pleased to discover that her fame could do good.

In 1890, Helen heard about a five-year-old boy named Tommy Stringer. The boy was blind and deaf, like Helen. After his parents died, he was placed in an institution in Philadelphia. Helen knew that Tommy could be educated and have a bright future if he could just get the chance to go to Perkins. However, Perkins was a very expensive school. With help from Annie, Helen started a fund-raising campaign. She wrote letters to friends and newspapers, asking for donations to help Tommy. Helen's campaign worked, and she was able to raise $1,600, which was a lot of money in those days and enough to send Tommy to Perkins. Annie was proud of Helen's accomplishment and her desire to help others. "I know she is destined to be the instrument of great good in the world," Annie wrote.

One day, Helen told Annie of a new goal she had her heart set on. She wanted to go to college. Some of her friends felt college would be too hard for Helen, and that she would be crushed by failure. But Helen refused to give up her dream.

She studied tirelessly for the entrance

examinations. Her printing by hand was slow, so Helen learned to use a typewriter. And she typed her answers through a nine-hour preliminary exam, plus a full-day final exam.

Helen did brilliantly. She won honors in English and German and was given credit in advanced Latin. Now her friends *had* to believe in her dream.

Helen entered Radcliffe College in the fall of 1900. This was a challenging experience for her. For the first time, Helen was attending school with students who could hear, see, and speak. No special steps were taken to make Helen's studies easier. At first, her textbooks were not available in Braille, so Annie had to read them all and spell every word into Helen's hand. Annie also attended all Helen's classes and spelled the teacher's lectures into Helen's hand. Later, Helen was able to get Braille textbooks, which made things a bit easier for both women.

Helen also faced loneliness and a lack of

acceptance at Radcliffe. Some of the teachers and administrators did not want her there. Only one teacher bothered to learn the manual alphabet so he could communicate directly with Helen. Helen also had few friends, because the other girls did not know how to communicate with her. Some of the students were also afraid to get to know Helen because she was famous. However, Helen kept working and remained cheerful. She was determined to overcome any obstacle in her path.

During her four years at Radcliffe, Helen found her life's work: to help others. She would tell the world her story. She would show everyone that the deaf and blind can learn. Helen wanted to bring hope to the handicapped. Her life was proof that everyone deserved a chance to learn.

CHAPTER 10:
An Amazing Life

In the years that followed, Helen wrote many books and magazine articles. Her most popular book was *The Story of My Life*, which was published in 1903. This biography was translated into fifty languages and became an international best seller.

Helen traveled around the world, speaking to people of all nations. Until Annie died, in 1936, she was with Helen every step of the way. Polly Thompson, a young Scottish woman, took Annie's place at Helen's side. And together, they carried on Helen's work.

During World War II, Helen visited soldiers who had been blinded in battle. She gave them courage and faith in the future. After the war, she worked with blind and deaf children. "I cannot stop to grow old while there is so much work to do," she said, "and so many children to help."

Helen received many awards for her work, including the Presidential Medal of Freedom. Until her death, on June 1, 1968, this most remarkable woman continued to give love, hope, and inspiration to thousands of human beings.

INDEX